IRREPARABLE HARM

RENATA ADLER

IRREPARABLE HARM
THE U.S. SUPREME COURT AND THE DECISION
THAT MADE GEORGE W. BUSH PRESIDENT

RENATA ADLER

MELVILLE HOUSE PUBLISHING
HOBOKEN, NEW JERSEY

This work appeared, in slightly altered form, in *The New Republic*,
July 30, 2001.

Book design: David Konopka

Melville House Publishing
P.O. Box 3278
Hoboken NJ 07030

mhpbooks.com

First Melville House printing 2004
Printed in the United States of America

ISBN:0-9749609-5-0
Library of Congress Cataloging-in-Publication Data

Adler, Renata.
  Irreparable harm : the U.S. Supreme Court and the decision that
made George W. Bush president / by Renata Adler.
     p. cm.
  "Originally published in *The new republic*, July 30, 2001."
  ISBN 0-9749609-5-0
  1. Political questions and judicial power--United States. 2.
Extraordinary remedies--United States. 3. United States. Supreme
Court. 4. Presidents--United States--Election--2000. I. New republic
(New York, N.Y.) II. Title.
  KF8748.A35 2004
  347.73'26--dc22
                                    2004013107

IN MEMORY OF
BURKE MARSHALL

IRREPARABLE HARM

"THE FRAMERS OF THE FEDERAL CONSTITUTION... VIEWED THE PRINCIPLE OF THE SEPARATION OF POWERS AS THE ABSOLUTELY CENTRAL GUARANTEE OF A JUST GOVERNMENT.... WITHOUT A SECURE STRUCTURE OF SEPARATED POWERS, OUR BILL OF RIGHTS WOULD BE WORTHLESS.... FREQUENTLY AN ISSUE OF THIS SORT WILL COME BEFORE THE COURT CLAD, SO TO SPEAK, IN SHEEP'S CLOTHING.... BUT THIS WOLF COMES AS A WOLF."

—JUSTICE ANTONIN SCALIA, DISSENT IN *MORRISON V. OLSON*, JUNE 29, 1988

"WHEN WE MAKE A DIFFICULT DECISION IN MANY AREAS—AND THIS WAS NOT THE MOST DIFFICULT DECISION THE COURT HAS MADE—.... [M]Y COLLEAGUES AND I WANT TO BE THE MOST TRUSTED PEOPLE IN AMERICA...."

—JUSTICE ANTHONY KENNEDY, TESTIMONY BEFORE THE HOUSE APPROPRIATIONS SUBCOMMITTEE, MARCH 29, 2001

1

Not infrequently, an event so radical that it alters everything appears for a time to have had no effect, or even not to have occurred. This is true in personal as in public life. A loss, a flood, a medical diagnosis, a rolling of tanks toward the statehouse—life goes on apparently as usual. Nothing is changed. It is particularly true of events that are irremediable. When there is nothing to be done, people go to work, eat their lunch, sleep, awaken to a vastly altered world, in ways that seem uncanny in their ordinariness. The decision of the Supreme Court in *Bush v. Gore*, in all three stages—accepting the case at all; reversing the judgment of the Florida State Supreme Court; above all, perhaps, granting a stay of the recount in Florida—gave rise to lots of comment. Outraged, gleeful, satisfied, resigned, the response seemed in almost every case to follow from the politics of the speaker. Republicans and "conservatives," for the most part, approved. Democrats and "liberals" did not. The decision seemed to close the subject. Normal life resumed. George W. Bush was president and that was that.

George W. Bush may become a distinguished president. As to the Court's "fundamental fairness" in the matter—its claim, as Justice Kennedy put it, on the people's "trust"—the issue seems settled in a single question: if Al Gore had been the petitioner, with the same set of facts and arguments brought by Bush, would the Court have decided as it did? A rhetorical question, surely. Not a single justice would have agreed to hear the case.

The major issue was never really who would become president, or even the immense damage that the Rehnquist Five have done to the integrity of the Court. Its moral, intellectual, and legal authority had already diminished over a long period of poorly reasoned opinions expressed in unseemly and unjudicial—often supercilious and even sneering—words. What remained was its power. The Supreme Court has made mistakes before: *Dred Scott, Plessy v. Ferguson, Korematsu*, and so on. What is unprecedented in *Bush v. Gore* is the exercise of power—specifically allocated by the Constitution to the states and to Congress, and specifically *not* to the federal judiciary—in the expression of a profound and absolute conflict of interest. The Rehnquist Five want the Court to become a self-selecting body. In their treatment of *Bush v. Gore*, they did what they could to achieve that result.

The decision, *per curiam*, unsigned, but apparently written by Justice Kennedy, with a separate concurrence by Justices Rehnquist, Scalia, and Thomas, is a swamp. No matter where you look at it, you find something specious, mischaracterized, incoherent, internally inconsistent, false. Because it issues from the Supreme Court, however, legal scholars, lawyers, judges, congressmen, voters, and senators—above all, senators—are obliged to take it seriously. Its consequences are serious in ways that have nothing, or almost nothing, to do with the election of George W. Bush. He would have become president in any case. If the hand count had gone, as it would probably have gone, for Al Gore, the procedures established in our system would have yielded two slates of electors from the state of Florida: one for Gore, one (submitted by the Republican Florida legislature) for Bush. Congress would have had to choose. If Congress could not agree, the

choice would revert to Florida to be made and certi-
fied by its executive, Governor Jeb Bush.

A disorderly process, certainly. It just happens
that some of the processes in our democracy are disorderly. The votes in all of the counties in all of the
fifty states, for example, are submitted and counted
by widely varying means. In Florida, the Supreme
Court found in this lack of uniformity a violation of
the equal protection clause. Just this once, just in
this case, just in this state, just on this day. The
equal protection claim was specious anyway. Just
who, if the counting had been permitted to continue,
was being denied the equal protection of the law? A
voter whose vote had already been tabulated by
machine? But that voter might be a Bush voter or a
Gore voter, and the votes being counted by hand, in
every county, might be Bush votes or Gore votes.
There might be disparate treatment, but there could
be no systematic or intentional disparate treatment,
favoring one candidate, or one voter, over another.
The standard for counting votes, in Florida as in
most other states, was "a clear indication of the
intent of the voter." This was not something that

needed to be "divined" or "discerned." A voter, even in chadless counties, who both checked and wrote in the name "Bush" or "Gore" on his ballot, had expressed his intent—in what was clearly a "legal vote." The machine would not count it. A manual recount would. The Supreme Court decision would disallow it.

In fact, both the decision and the concurrence express disdain for the legal standard, in Florida and in so many other states. Why, Justice O'Connor asked irritably during the oral arguments, could these voters not follow "clear instructions"? The concurrence actually devotes many lines to this sort of argument: "Florida law cannot reasonably be thought to require the counting of *improperly marked ballots*.... Each precinct... provides *instructions on how properly to cast a vote*"—as though voting were some form of test, which those aspiring to vote might pass or fail. The concurrence derides voters who cast "ballots that are not *marked in the manner* that these voting instructions explicitly and prominently specify"—in contrast to the machines, which perform "precisely in the manner designed."

(The machines performed, as it happened, poorly, and in some locations not at all.) Any other position, the concurrence goes on, in the diction that has become one of the Rehnquist Five's defining characteristics, "is of course absurd."

The difficulty remains: the standard for a "legal vote" is not an IQ test, or a test of classroom behavior that requires people to behave "properly" or to follow "instructions." (The "instructions" in some counties, anyway, told the voter to make sure to "cast a vote on every page." An unfortunate instruction: Any voter who followed it would have produced an "overvote," which the machine would disallow.) The accusatory, punitive, even contemptuous dismissal of voters whom the Court apparently deems too stupid to be allowed to vote at all (echoes here of the "literacy test" that used to accompany the poll tax in the South) dismisses as well what is, in Florida and most other states, the law: the test is, inescapably, the "intent of the voter." It was according to this standard that the manual recount was proceeding when the Court brought it to a halt.

2

The trouble with a swamp of a decision is that even to deal with it is to be drawn into it. The four dissents politely and eloquently demolished every element of both the decision and the concurrence, to the degree those elements could be articulated. Almost all subsequent commentary, whether in article or book form, demolished them in more detail. But always in ways that seem contingent. Some distinguished commentators have suggested that, if the Bush presidency turns out well, the decision will be vindicated. Or they have pointed out that when the Supreme Court has made mistakes before, it has with time corrected them. Or even that the real precedent for this judicial aberration was *Roe v. Wade*, when the Court made a decision that might, they felt, have been better left to Congress or the states. But all of them, I think, understate the gravity of what has happened, and its possible consequences for at least a generation.

To return for a moment to the decision—in particular, to Justice Scalia's concurrence (in itself unusual) in the Supreme Court's order, which abruptly halted the manual count by granting

Bush's application for a stay. It is often forgotten that, in addition to Florida's state courts, lawyers for Bush had already brought their case before three *federal* courts (the U.S. District Courts of Orlando and Miami, and the U.S. Court of Appeals for the Eleventh Circuit Court in Atlanta), without success. A "stay" is a form of the ancient equitable remedy of injunction. Centuries ago, a petitioner might appeal directly to the king for a writ to "enjoin" his neighbor from doing something so drastic and destructive that it threatened the petitioner with "irreparable harm," damage, in other words, that could not subsequently be undone or compensated. The very basis of a petition for such a writ was an emergency.

A "stay"—and every application by petitioners Bush and Cheney in the federal courts to stop the manual recount was phrased in terms of "An Emergency Motion" or "An Emergency Application for a Stay"—is a drastic remedy. It is not to be granted unless the petitioner clearly establishes that he will suffer "irreparable injury" if the stay is denied; and that this threatened injury outweighs whatever damage the proposed injunction may cause the opposing party. He must also establish that granting a stay would not be adverse to the public interest.

In his concurrence, Justice Scalia did not trouble for a moment to consider whether the threatened injury to Bush if the counting continued outweighed the damage to Gore if it did not. Scalia went straight to "irreparable harm." If the manual count continued, he said, it "does in my view threaten irreparable harm to the petitioner, and to the country, by casting a cloud upon what he claims to be the legitimacy of his election."

Well, there it is. The irreparable harm of "casting a cloud." In the long and honorable tradition of injunctions and stays, this "irreparable injury" is a new one. Not just a cloud, but a cloud on "what he claims to be the legitimacy" of what he is claiming. By that standard, of course, every litigant in every case should be granted an injunction to halt the proceeding that offends him: The prosecutor casts a cloud on a claim of innocence; the civil plaintiff, a cloud on the defendant's claim that he has already paid him. And of course vice versa, the defendants casting clouds on plaintiffs and prosecutors. The whole adversary system consists of a casting of clouds.

Justice Scalia's choice of words seems derived, perhaps intentionally, from the laws of property: "cloud on title"—with, perhaps, an overtone of libel. As though a vote were a form of speech, unprotected by the First Amendment, and the counting of votes were, in some sense, defamatory and damaging to the candidate's reputation. But from tort claims to suits in antitrust, legal process virtually consists of this casting of clouds on claims of legitimacy. Perhaps all of them should be halted or enjoined.

Whatever "cloud" Scalia had in mind—and it seems to be emotional (anxiety perhaps, or the state of being miffed)—the "harm" to Bush could not possibly be "irreparable," since it was entirely within the power of the Court, or the manual count itself, to dispel it. If the count went for Bush, no cloud at all. If it went for Gore, the Court would have time to deem the results, if the Court so found, invalid. If the count went Gore's way, and the Court found no fault with it, the process would have gone just as the

Constitution and our political tradition provided that it should, as though the Court had never entered the process—where it did not, in any event, belong.

Scalia's argument for the stay obviously did not "clearly establish" any, let alone all four, of the requirements for the remedy. His finding of "irreparable harm" was so obviously unserious that even the *per curiam* did not bother with it. Here is how, retroactively, the *per curiam* justified its halting of the count: "Given the Court's assessment that the recount process underway was probably being conducted in an unconstitutional manner, the Court stayed the order."

"Given," "probably being conducted," "unconstitutional manner": This is not language on which to base an order for a stay. It is not language on which to base a decision of any kind. The word "probably" alone defeats the argument: The courts have always held that no stay will issue if the harm is "speculative." And the *per curiam* babbles vaguely on. The mandate of the Florida Supreme Court "is not well calculated to sustain the confidence that all citizens must have in the outcome of elections"; it "jeopardizes the legislative wish"; it "frustrates a legislative desire"; "a legislative wish... would counsel... against any construction that Congress might deem"—all these hypotheticals, wishes, frustrations, desires; what a "wish... would counsel... against," what Congress "might deem." The Court, when it speaks honorably, speaks in straight declaratory sentences. It speaks not of legislative wishes, but of commands; not of what Congress might deem, but of what it has said, enacted, or required.

Here is Scalia, waffling, with a little joke based on Alice: "Count first, and rule upon legality afterwards, is not a recipe for producing elections that have the public acceptance democratic stability requires." Recipe. The public acceptance democratic stability requires. Well calculated to sustain the confidence that all citizens must have in the outcome. All this is not just arguable, and certainly not before the Court. It is not the Court's business. As it happens, count (or take any action which the law does not specifically forbid) first, and rule upon legality afterwards, is precisely the basis of our free and entrepreneurial system. It is one of the reasons constitutional law requires the Court to consider only specific "cases and controversies" (in contrast to abstract, hypothetical, or contingent questions) and prohibits the Court from issuing what are called "advisory opinions." Halt the count, and rule upon legality beforehand, is presumably the "recipe" for producing the kind of elections (those "that have the public acceptance democratic stability requires") that Scalia has in mind.

But none of this, not a word or a concept, is the reasoning or the language of the law. And the vague, nattering—simultaneously brazen, timid, and evasive—quality of the decision culminates, of course, in this: "Our consideration is limited to the present circumstances, for the problem of equal protection in election processes generally presents many complexities."

Look at that sentence a minute. What can it possibly mean? It apparently *says* that, for some reason, the decision in *Bush v. Gore* is not to be regarded as precedent for any other. But if this were so, it would undermine, at one stroke, the whole

29

basis of American and Anglo-Saxon law. That each case has precedential value, *must* have precedential value, is the bedrock of our system of justice. Otherwise each case can be decided ad hoc, at the caprice of judges—non-elected, federal judges with lifelong tenure. The Constitution and even the Magna Carta would be superseded, the justices would be kings.

It is, however, simply not in the power of the Court to determine that its decision has no precedential value. All decisions of the Court have such value, though it is hard to see how this particular travesty could serve as precedent for anything—or, for that matter, how it could be abandoned or overruled. But a special case, with no precedents and no future applications, is a case that, for ancient, profound, and lasting reasons, no court under our system is entitled to decide. No court has a right to say, This case is the law, crafted for one citizen, George W. Bush, and for him alone.

Linda Greenhouse, in *The New York Times* two days after the decision, got it just right. "Among the most baffling aspects of the opinion," she wrote, "was its simultaneous creation of a new equal protection right not to have ballots counted according to different standards and its disclaimer that this new constitutional principle would ever apply in another case." The "new constitutional principle" never could apply in another case, because it does not and could not exist. It would disallow every election in the country—in the history of the country. The Platonic ideal of a voting machine that the chief justice seems to envision, "precisely designed" to create uniform standards nationwide, does not exist either. If it did, the Court would have no power to impose it. Nor would Congress. The notion of machines, "precisely designed" and even of "uniform standards nationwide," raises the question of who, or what, designs, imposes, and oversees them. And the necessary centralization of power and order that this implies is precisely the way nations lose the power to vote.

In *Bush v. Gore*, the citation of "precedents" that are not precedents, particularly civil rights cases (*NAACP v. Alabama*, for example, or *Bouie v.*

31

City of Columbia, a 1964 case involving black sit-in demonstrators: "What we would do in the present case," the concurrence says, "is *precisely parallel*") conveys the degree of disingenuousness and spite that has so frequently characterized Rehnquist's opinions. His tone in the majority has perhaps carried over from the years when he was most bitterly in dissent. Justice Ginsburg dealt with this sort of citation. The Florida Supreme Court, in its finding that "counting every legal vote" was the "overriding concern" of Florida's Election Code, "surely should not be bracketed with state high courts of the Jim Crow South." She dealt with the chief justice's other "casual citations" as well, pointing out how few and inapposite they were.

There is also, in the decision, an unusually high measure of hypocrisy, particularly in its affectation of helplessness: "None are more conscious of the vital limits on judicial authority than are the members of this Court.... However, it becomes our *unsought responsibility to resolve*... issues the judicial system has been *forced to confront*" and so forth. (In hearings before the House Appropriations Committee in March, Justice Kennedy, along with his remarks about "trust," actually pointed out, in defense of the *per curiam*, that it was not the justices who filed the suit.) Apart from outright misrepresentations of the law, there are several gratuitously insulting comparisons between Katherine Harris and the Florida Supreme Court ("The Florida Supreme Court, although it must defer to the Secretary's interpretations,... rejected her reasonable interpretation and embraced the peculiar one") and myriad inconsistencies. The decision, which has just said that the state court "must defer to the Secretary's interpretations," suddenly pretends that it confronts "a state court with the *power to assure uniformity*" in vote counts—a "power" that the Florida Supreme Court manifestly lacks.

And there are, at the core, some outright lies. Even the statement that seven justices of the court essentially agree, for example, and that "the only disagreement is as to the remedy," is false. The two justices whom the majority tries to embrace, Souter and Breyer, begin their dissents with clear statements

33

that the Court should not have taken the case, that it was wrong to grant a stay, and that the decision itself is wrong. That puts rather a lot of weight on the "only." Souter and Breyer did try to salvage something from the debacle by giving the Florida Supreme Court another chance to meet even the most specious arguments of the *per curiam*. But the majority, with its own agenda, would not permit even this.

It is not enough to say that this is the most lawless decision in the history of the Court. People have said, Well, somebody had to decide what the outcome of the election was, one way or the other. But somebody *was* deciding (or rather had decided) it: the voters. If the outcome remained in doubt, Congress would decide, or remit the choice to the Executive of the state. Others have said that we were approaching chaos, a constitutional crisis, that only the Supreme Court, in its robes and its wisdom, could resolve. But there was no constitutional crisis, except the one of the Supreme Court's own creation. The events in Florida and the unfolding story were in fact a kind of political thriller. Voters were rather enjoying the suspense, when the

Court, for its own reasons, jumped right in to stop the contest, so as to ensure that no one, ever, would find out the score.

What does it matter? The system has always been strong enough to withstand mistakes of every kind, poor policies and choices, corrupt administrations, bad judgments on the part of elected and electorate alike, bad laws, unjust verdicts, rigged elections, miscounted votes, and bad decisions by malign or misguided courts. In *Chapters of Erie*, still the best work of muckraking in our history, Charles F. Adams Jr. and Henry Adams devoted many chapters to the corruption of the courts. But there is something different about *Bush v. Gore*.

3

It has now become clear that the recent case is only the latest and most extreme in a series of cases, *Morrison v. Olson, Clinton v. Jones*, and the initial remand to the Florida Supreme Court for "clarification." And it was Antonin Scalia, in his dissent in *Morrison v. Olson*, who gave us the clearest indication of what has happened here and what is really at stake. Morrison v. Olson, decided in 1988, was the case in which the Supreme Court overruled the Court of Appeals for the District of Columbia, and upheld, as constitutional, the Ethics in Government Act of 1978, which established the office of independent counsel. Justices Brennan, Blackmun, and Marshall were still members of that Court, but Scalia's was the sole dissent. His opinion was eloquent and well reasoned, and he alone was right. It was as though the justices, and everyone else who should have known better, were not paying attention.

Scalia pointed out that, under the act, the independent counsel, or special prosecutor, would have virtually unlimited power—scope, discretion, funds, staff, tenure. He quoted at length from a great speech by Justice Robert Jackson, delivered in 1940, when he was still attorney general, about

the temptations and the duties of *any* prosecutor,
his vast powers and immense discretion, and the
dangers of abusing them—specifically, by not
"discovering the commission of a crime and then
looking for the man who has committed it," but
"picking the man" and then "putting investigators
to work, to pin some offense on him." Any prosecutor, Jackson said, "stands a fair chance of finding at
least a technical violation of some act on the part of
almost anyone," and then "the real crime becomes
that of being unpopular with the predominant or
governing group, being attached to the wrong
political views, or being personally obnoxious."

Jackson's speech, and Scalia's opinion, con-
tained a virtual blueprint of what the independent
counsel's office, under Kenneth Starr, would
become and do. But Scalia's main argument was
that the Ethics in Government Act so seriously violated the constitutional separation of powers,
which, for very good reasons, vests *all* the Executive
power (including the power of prosecution) in the
president, that it violated "the absolutely central

guarantee of a just Government." "The purpose of the separation and equilibration of powers," Scalia said, "and of the unitary Executive in particular, was not merely to assure effective government but to preserve individual freedom." When the Court upholds as constitutional a law that creates a prosecutor outside the Executive, "this is not the government of laws that the Constitution established; it is not a government of laws at all." "That the Court could hold otherwise demonstrates the wisdom of our former constitutional system."

The warning was apt and it was prescient, but Scalia thought that the greatest danger wrought by this diminution of the Executive would come from the legislative branch. "The statute," he wrote, "is acrid with the smell of impeachment." Also, "this is an open invitation for Congress to experiment. The possibilities are endless, and the Court does not understand what the separation of powers, what 'ambition… countering ambition'… is all about, if it does not expect Congress to try them."

Congress, of course, did "try them," and the independent counsel himself set off the debacle of an impeachment process. But what I had not realized, what nobody so far as I know has pointed out, was a provision of the act that the majority in *Morrison* virtually relegates to a footnote. "Most importantly," Justice Rehnquist said, speaking for the Court, "the Act vests in the Special Division the power to choose who will serve as independent counsel and the power to define his or her jurisdiction." It is only Footnote Three that tells us what the newly created "Special Division" is to be. It "consists of three circuit court judges or justices appointed by the Chief Justice of the United States." The chief justice was, as he still is, Justice Rehnquist.

The wisdom of this arrangement is applauded in Footnote Thirteen: "Indeed, in light of judicial experience with prosecutors in criminal cases, it could be said that courts are especially well qualified to appoint prosecutors." If that doesn't give you a little chill, it may still shed light on the scene of the man in his Iolanthe-inspired robe presiding so affably in the Senate over a trial set in motion by a special prosecutor, whom he had selected and supervised.

Scalia's dissent in *Morrison* demolished the majority opinion delivered by Chief Justice Rehnquist. "The prospect is frightening," Scalia wrote, and there is nothing sarcastic, or insincere, in the tone of this opinion. "The fairness of a process must be adjudged on the basis of what it permits to happen." The appointment of "the mini-Executive that is the independent counsel," a prosecutor outside the Executive Branch, unelected and accountable to no one, destroyed "the equilibrium... the Founding Fathers envisioned when they established a Chief Executive accountable to the people." Above all, it destroyed the tension among the three branches, which limits the power of each and provides the "absolutely central guarantee of a just government." "That is what this suit is about. Power. The allocation of power... in such fashion as to preserve the equilibrium the Constitution sought to establish. Frequently an issue of this sort will come before the Court clad, so to speak, in sheep's clothing: the potential of the asserted principle to effect important change in the equilibrium of power is not immediately evident.... But this wolf comes as a wolf." The only thing that Scalia seemed less than prescient about was which branch was going to "experiment." The danger came not from the legislative but from the judiciary, not from Congress but from the Supreme Court.

In case after case since *Morrison*, the Court, with majorities that now include Scalia, has expressed its disdain for the other branches, for elective officials of every kind (now including, of course, state judges), for voters, for colleagues on the Court who are not members of the Rehnquist Five. The diction of those five has been marked by an overwhelming sense of their own superiority, while the quality of their reasoning and of their decisions has radically declined. In 1997, there was *Clinton v. Jones*, decided by a unanimous Court. It seemed for a time that even the best of the justices were asleep, or had lost contact with life in the outside world. The decision refused to stay the trial of Paula Jones's claims against President Clinton. The district judge had allowed discovery to go forward, but had concluded that an immediate trial, which "might hamper the President in conducting the duties of his office," could be postponed until the end of his term.

The Supreme Court held otherwise. While it might "consume some of the President's time and attention," a trial "appears to us highly unlikely to occupy any substantial amount of [his] time," or to impose an "unacceptable burden on [his] time and energy." There was also no "perceptible" or "serious" risk that a "trial might generate unrelated civil actions" that could "conceivably hamper the President" in the conduct of his office. Meanwhile Jones's "interest in bringing the case to trial" and the "timely vindication of her most fundamental rights" should not be subject to delay. "Delaying trial would increase the danger of prejudice resulting from the loss of evidence, including the inability of witnesses to recall specific facts, or the possible death of a party." Such a delay, because of the "unforeseeable loss of evidence" and so forth, would subject Jones to a "risk of irreparable harm."

So urgent was Jones's complaint that she did not file it until two days before the three-year deadline under the statute of limitations. Her claim at the time consisted of four parts: violation of her civil rights under state law; conspiracy to violate her civil rights under federal law; intentional infliction

45

of emotional distress; and defamation. The Court's decision was certainly one of its least wise and prescient. What links it to *Bush v. Gore* (apart from considerable overlap among the authors of the briefs for Jones and Bush) is the question of a "stay" and "irreparable harm." The trial of Jones must not be stayed, even temporarily, because the delay may cause Jones irreparable harm. (The Supreme Court here seems out of touch even with the experience of ordinary citizens before the courts: there is *always* delay, with its attendant risks of loss of evidence, and so on.) But the manual count in the Florida counties *must*, permanently, be stayed, because of the risk of irreparable harm to—well, to George W. Bush. The combination of *Jones* and *Morrison* was nearly the destruction of the Executive.

4

And there we are. One risk that seems to have passed, until now, under the radar of some of the justices is that the extreme right has become adept at using politically correct buzzwords (words from civil rights cases, from feminism, from affirmative action, from multiculturalism, and so forth) to advance diametrically opposite agendas. With *Bush v. Gore*, the majority of the Court—in spite of the persuasiveness and the eloquence of the dissents, and the efforts of the dissenting justices to preserve somehow the continuity of the institution—has virtually parodied the history and the meaning of such words ("equal protection" is but one example) to become quite openly the most dangerous branch. It has simply taken over, almost casually seizing rights that belong to the state courts, Congress, the electorate, and defying anyone to do something about it.

And it is far from clear what can be done about it. Manual counting of the votes is now, even as a matter of history, meaningless. Many votes had already vanished by the time *The Miami Herald* started counting them; and more will surely change or disappear before the *New York Times* consortium is done. The election of Bush was never the real problem. The assertion of power—in a matter in which the Court is morally and constitutionally precluded from playing any part—is. The justices serve for life. They have now acted, in their judicial capacity, to promote their choice of a man who will select their colleagues and successors, who will also serve for life. The losses—of trust in the Court, of respect for the law, and of belief in the vote itself—are almost the least of it. The only citizens who can do anything about it are the president (who has already made clear his ideological preferences, and who is now also compromised and in their debt) and the members of the Senate. The line is drawn. Of course, surprises are always possible. But there can be no more lapses of attention, no more confirmations of ideological clones in ethnically mixed disguises, no more ideologues at all.

The difficulty, even the danger, is profound. It is embodied, after all, in that apparently harmless little shrug of a sentence about the decision being limited to the "present circumstances." If you once cede to the Court the power to decide elections, let alone even the power to halt counting of the votes, then you have ceded it everything. It is no use for the justices to claim that this case has no precedential value. The "just this once" promise is disingenuous on its face—especially in the "present circumstances." Every decision of the Court, under our system, becomes precedent; there is nothing to keep some future Court from responding in the same way, halting (on grounds of equal protection or whatever other specious grounds), in every county and in every state, a vote which displeases the majority of the Court. And there is no appeal.

This is by no means an unlikely consequence. What the Court says is the law *is* the law, until the Court itself says otherwise. The only leash on the Court, until now, was the Court's own history—its continuity as an institution that relies on precedent, reasoning, good faith, tradition, and its place among the three branches of government and within the federal system. It has now, with every affectation of helplessness, slipped that leash. There is no explanation in *Bush v. Gore* that can fit within the function of the Supreme Court, no rational explanation of this arbitrary exercise of power, in the language that the Supreme Court has always used to explain what it does. And all those affectations of helplessness—what it was "compelled" or "forced" to do, those "unsought" responsibilities it "could not abdicate"—were coupled with expressions of immense self-satisfaction.

There seems, really, no question about it. This is a turning point. Not because of its effect on this election or on the status of the Court or on the people's trust. Least of all was it a simple matter of choosing between two candidates in a close presidential election. Almost all the books, articles, and commentaries about it have, in one way or another, been useful—particularly *Bush v. Gore: The Court Cases and the Commentary*, in that it includes so many of the actual court decisions. Most critics speak of damage to the Court itself; most supporters speak in terms of excusing little faults, in view of what they seem to regard as a rescue of the system from "chaos." Almost all speak as though there were some continuity between this decision and the entire history of the Court. But there is no continuity. The legacy of this Court is disaster—which no façade of collegiality, or relatively cuddly subsequent decisions, can conceal or rectify.

One outcome of this case seems almost certain. Having once intervened to effect the outcome of the electoral process (which it had neither the authority, nor the competence, nor as it turned out even the good faith to decide), the Court—under this Rehnquist or another, with the concurrence of this Kennedy and O'Connor or others—will try again, relying on (perhaps even "refining") the ineradicable precedent of *Bush v. Gore*. As Scalia put it, in 1988, in *Morrison*:

> Evidently the governing standard is to be what might be called the unfettered wisdom of a majority of this Court, revealed to an obedient people on a case-by-case basis. This is not only not the government of laws that the Constitution established; it is not a government of laws at all.

And:

What if [the judges] are partisan, as judges have been known to be.... There is no remedy for that, not even a political one. Judges after all have life tenure.

And:

The Court essentially says "trust us...." I think the Constitution gives... the people more protection than that.

And finally:

That the Court could possibly conclude otherwise demonstrates both the wisdom of our former constitutional system... and the folly of the new system of standardless judicial allocation of powers we adopt today.

Scalia was writing, of course, only of the act that established the office of independent counsel. But he had at length quoted Jackson, for whom Rehnquist had clerked—and whose views Rehnquist has often managed, from the day of his confirmation hearings to this day, to misrepresent. Scalia's dissent even denounced, as an unconstitutional breach of the separation of powers, the special division that Rehnquist would head. The act which established the office of the special prosecutor, and which the Rehnquist Court upheld as constitutional, led to one disaster after another. Now it is the judiciary that has accepted the "invitation," under *Morrison*, to "experiment" with "possibilities."

The Court, even when it acts on a lawless basis, is beyond appeal. Our system provides for the lower courts no equivalent of civil disobedience, or jury nullification, or even the degree of freedom enjoyed by dissident prelates within the Church. It is not entirely inconceivable that even the lower federal courts will (in spite of Justice Kennedy's vague and unenforceable disclaimer) invoke *Bush v. Gore* to halt counts or otherwise intervene in elections. The damage is done, and cannot ever be quite undone. But it can be limited. If the Senate exercises, with the utmost care, its constitutional responsibility to advise and consent, *Bush v. Gore* really will with the passage of time have been just a radical aberration. If the Court succeeds, however, in having allocated to itself powers that belong to the states and to the other branches—and if the Senate's examination of any candidate for a federal court is in the least perfunctory—the tanks have really rolled. The Founding Fathers, who did after all vote by hand, will have left us a wonderful form of government, which we somehow permitted the Court to throw away.

AFTERWORD

Two months after this piece was published, there was the disaster of 9/11 and, in its aftermath, the passage of legislation which does not so much grant the Court even greater powers as fuse the powers of the three branches into a single power, the prosecutiorial—of which Justice Scalia, quoting Justice Robert Jackson, once so eloquently warned. The Solicitor General of the United States, as it happens, is now Theodore Olson, the Olson of *Morrison v. Olson*, the case in which Scalia alone was right, in warning of the threat the establishment of the office of special prosecutor posed to the entire constitutional sytem. "The Court essentially says 'trust us,'" he wrote. "I think the Constitution gives ... the people more protection than that." Much of what government has said, since the events of 9/11, has been a variant of "trust us."

The doctrine of Preemption, in international affairs, amounts to a variant of injunction in drastic military form. The questions—whether the preempting nation will otherwise suffer irreparable injury; whether that injury outweighs whatever damage the preemption itself might cause; and whether the preemption will not be adverse to the public interest—are much the same. There has, of course, been nothing inherently violent in the ancient equitable remedy of injunction. And a real injunction can issue only from a court, or other neutral tribunal. (In at least two cases now before the Supreme Court, the administration actually argues that the president, the military, even Intelligence "Interrogators" are, under recent law, just such "neutral" tribunals, which can be trusted like any other court; the cases reached the Court at about the same time photographs of the work of Interrogators came out of Abu Ghraib.)

In his dissent in *Morrison*, in 1988, Justice Scalia wrote, with some bitterness, of "the wisdom of our former constitutional system." In *Bush v. Gore*, decided four years ago, the balance of powers which sustains that system was radically undermined. Now, under vastly more critical circumstances, there is another national election. Whatever the outcome, and whether or not any court will intervene, the fusion of all powers in a single prosecutorial power, of unprecedented scope and almost limitless discretion, is sure to test the Court again. Whether we are already speaking of our "former constitutional system" will depend in great part on what that Court decides.

—Renata Adler, 2004

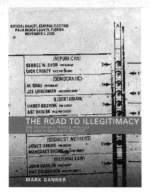

THE ROAD TO ILLEGITIMACY
One Reporter's Travels Through
the 2000 Florida Vote Recount
Mark Danner

0-9749609-6-9
$8.95 US / $12.95 CAN

In a masterful work of investigative journalism, *New Yorker* staffer Mark Danner looks into the tense counting and recounting of votes in Florida with a revealing on-the-scene account of the near-hysterical partisan bickering over each and every ballot. What he uncovers is shocking—and his riveting account is a sobering consideration of the question the Supreme Court left hanging: Who actually got the most votes?

IRREPARABLE HARM
The U.S. Supreme Court and the Decision
That Made George W. Bush President
Renata Adler

0-9749609-5-0
$8.95 US / $12.95 CAN

In a blistering, no-holds-barred analysis, acclaimed writer Renata Adler uncovers numerous problems with the Supreme Court's decision in *Bush v. Gore*. Adler, herself an attorney, uncovers instances where the judges seem to have miscited their own previous decisions... examines what was said by attorneys and judges in the courtroom... and, ultimately, reveals what really happened in this historic case.

THE BIG CHILL
The Great, Unreported Story of
the Bush Inauguration Protest
Dennis Loy Johnson

0-9749609-7-7
$8.95 US / $12.95 CAN

An enormous, angry crowd lined the parade route for George Bush's inauguration, causing him to abandon the traditional walk along Pennsylvania Avenue. Yet a photo of a walking Bush appeared in newspapers the next day. In a gripping first-hand report, Johnson reveals what really happened in Washington: the enormous military presence, the violence between police and protestors, how the Bush photo was staged—and why the historic protest was ignored.